THAT'S SO WEIRD!

PAMELA KENNEDY
and ANNE KENNEDY BRADY

Worthy kids
ideals®

ISBN-13: 978-1-945470-45-5

Published by WorthyKids/Ideals, an imprint of Worthy Publishing Group, a division of Worthy Media, Inc.,
in association with Museum of the Bible.

Copyright © 2018 by Museum of the Bible, Inc
409 3rd St. SW
Washington, D.C. 20024-4706
Museum of the Bible is an innovative, global, educational institution whose purpose
is to invite all people to engage with the history, narrative, and impact of the Bible.

Library of Congress CIP data is on file

Unless otherwise indicated, scripture quotations are from the ESV® Bible (The Holy Bible, English Standard Version®),
copyright © 2001 by Crossway, a publishing ministry of Good News Publishers. Used by permission. All rights reserved.

Produced with the assistance of Hudson Bible (www.HudsonBible.com)
Illustrations by Aliaksei Zhuro

Printed and bound in the U.S.A.
LSC-Craw_Feb18_1

GUESS WHO?

Do you know who spent six years hiding from an evil queen?
Can you name the girl who got a whole year of free beauty treatments?
Or what about the ancient superhero who pushed down
a temple with his bare hands?

The pages of the Bible are filled with weird and wonderful stories about
men, women, boys, and girls who did amazing things. You won't believe
some of the strange and interesting facts about both well-known
and little-known people in the Bible.

That's So Weird! contains trivia about more than 100 Bible figures
and tells you where in the Bible (book, chapter, and verse) you can read
more about them. We used the Protestant edition of the Bible, which
has 66 books in the Old and New Testaments.

You'll be amazed to learn more about some of your favorite people in
the Bible. And you'll learn some surprising facts about others too!
Turn the page to dive in and have some fun!

CHECK YOUR LUGGAGE!

Saul

didn't want to be Israel's **first king,** so he **hid** in a **PILE OF BAGGAGE.**

(1 Samuel 10:20–22)

NOAH had
hundreds of animals
on the ark, but only
7 other people to
help out.

(Genesis 7:7–9)

Pass the pooper-scooper!

Jonah spent **3 days** and **3 nights** inside a **huge fish.** Then the fish **vomited** Jonah up on the beach—**alive!** (Jonah 1:17, 2:10)

Do you **play** an instrument? **Jubal** is the first musician named in the Bible.

(Genesis 4:21)

When **Jesus** was born, his parents used the animals' feeding trough for his crib!

(Luke 2:6–7)

Surf's up!

PETER

once stepped out of a boat and

WALKED

ON TOP OF THE WATER.

(Matthew 14:29)

DOUBLE TROUBLE!

Isaac and **Rebekah** were the parents of the **first twins** in the Bible, **Esau** and **Jacob.**

(Genesis 25:24–26)

Samson's supernatural strength allowed him to **push down a Philistine temple** with his bare hands.

(Judges 16:29–30)

When
God offered
Solomon
anything he wanted,
Solomon asked for wisdom.
you
What would
ask for?

(2 Chronicles 1:7–10)

A servant girl named

Rhoda

became so excited to hear

Peter

knocking on the door

that she forgot to

LET HIM IN!

(Acts 12:13–14)

Paul's nephew **overheard a plot** to **assassinate** his uncle and warned him, **saving his life.**

(Acts 23:12–32)

How did **Isaac** choose his bride? A servant chose **Rebekah** for him because she offered to give water to **10** thirsty camels.

(Genesis 24:10–20)

When **Moses** was born, his mother was afraid **he'd be killed,** so she put him in a **waterproof basket** AND HID HIM ON A RIVERBANK.

(Exodus 2:1–3)

Sweet!

Ezekiel

had a **vision** that he **ate a paper scroll.** He said it **tasted like honey.**

(Ezekiel 3:3)

19

ABRAHAM AND SARAH

laughed when they were told they would **HAVE A BABY.**

When the baby was born, they named him

ISAAC

which means **"he laughs."**

(Genesis 17:17, 19; 18:12)

When Balaam

got mad at his **donkey** and beat her with a stick, the donkey **spoke up** and **asked** why she was

BEING MISTREATED!

(Numbers 22:28)

21

Pharaoh's daughter

found **baby Moses** in the river. She adopted him and **raised him as her son.**

(Exodus 2:5–10)

Saul's friends once saved his life by hiding him in a basket and lowering him through an opening in the city walls.

(Acts 9:23–25)

Jacob loved a beautiful shepherdess named **Rachel.** Her father tricked Jacob into working for him for

14 YEARS

in order to marry her!

(Genesis 29:18–30)

You GO, girl!

Miriam, Moses and Aaron's sister, is the first **FEMALE LEADER** mentioned in the Bible.

(Exodus 15:20–21; Micah 6:4)

A woman named **Jael** killed **Sisera**, an enemy commander, WITH A TENT PEG. Jael saved her people from **destruction.**

(Judges 4:21)

Aaron,

the brother of Moses,
was so beloved
that when he died
the Hebrew people cried for

30 DAYS.

(Numbers 20:29)

King Og's iron bed was so big you could fit a Volkswagen Beetle on it!

(Deuteronomy 3:11)

Joseph's older brothers got **so mad** at him that they **sold him to slave traders** and pretended he had been **attacked by an animal!**

(Genesis 37:18–28)

The first **song** described in the Bible came from **Moses** and  **AFTER THEY ESCAPED FROM EGYPT.**

(Exodus 15:1–21)

Shiphrah and Puah

were Hebrews who helped women give birth. They lied to the Egyptian king in order to save Hebrew babies.

(Exodus 1:15–19)

SAMSON told this **riddle.**

See if you can solve it:

"Out of the **eater** came **something** to eat. Out of the **strong** came something **sweet!**"

(Judges 14:8,14)

ANSWER: Samson once found a beehive dripping with honey in a dead lion!

33

HELLO
my name is

Eve

Eve, the first woman, was named by her husband, **Adam.** Adam named the animals too! (Genesis 3:20)

Ehud was the only **LEFT-HANDED JUDGE,** and he killed a king with a **hidden knife.**

(Judges 3:15–21)

There was a **woman** from **En-dor** who could **bring up** the **spirits of the dead.**

Boo!

(1 Samuel 28:7)

SHHHHH!

Rahab hid two **Israelite spies** on the **roof** of her house all day. That night, she helped them escape down the side of the city wall on a rope.

(Joshua 2:1, 15)

Samson once caught

300

foxes,

TIED TORCHES TO THEIR TAILS,

and let them loose

to burn down

his enemy's crops.

(Judges 15:4–5)

GOD TOLD the prophet

Ezekiel

to **bake bread** over a fire made from

human poop!

(Ezekiel 4:12)

On one
of the only snowy
days mentioned in
the Bible, Benaiah went
down into a pit and killed
a lion. That'll give you
GOOSEBUMPS!

(2 Samuel 23:20)

The 3 oldest people mentioned in the Bible
are Methuselah (969 years old),
Jared (962 years old), and Noah (950 years old)!

(Genesis 5:20, 27; 9:29)

When **Moses** came down

from **Mt. Sinai**

with the tablets containing the

Ten Commandments,

his face **glowed** so brightly

that people were afraid

TO LOOK AT HIM.

(Exodus 34:29–30)

Gideon's army of **300** men were armed only with **trumpets, torches, and empty jugs** when they defeated **135,000** enemy soldiers!

(Judges 7:16–22)

43

Sssssssstrange!

Aaron once threw

his **staff** on the **ground,**

AND IT TURNED

into a snake.

(Exodus 7:8–13)

Samuel was raised **in the temple** by a priest named **Eli.** He only saw his mother **once a year,** when she brought him a **new coat!**

(1 Samuel 2:18–19)

KING SAUL wanted to **kill David,** but David's best friend, **JONATHAN,** saved him with a **SECRET SIGN.**

(1 Samuel 20:18–23)

BFF!

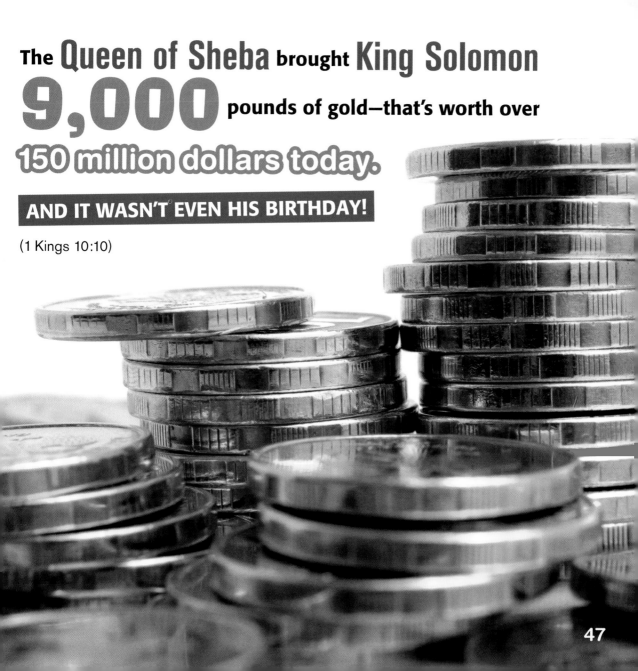

The **Queen of Sheba** brought **King Solomon** **9,000** pounds of gold—that's worth over **150 million dollars today.**

AND IT WASN'T EVEN HIS BIRTHDAY!

(1 Kings 10:10)

Deborah, the only female judge mentioned in the Bible, held court under a palm tree.

(Judges 4:4–5)

After his **death,** the prophet **Samuel** was **called up** from beyond the grave by **Saul,** and Samuel had **bad news** for Saul.

THAT'S SPOOKY!

(1 Samuel 28:3, 14–19)

49

JOSHUA ordered his followers to **shout** and **BLOW TRUMPETS,** and the walls of **Jericho** **CAME CRASHING DOWN.**

(Joshua 6:20)

When he was **just a teenager,** **David** defeated **Goliath,** a **9-foot-tall giant,** by hitting him on the **forehead** with one **smooth stone.**

(1 Samuel 17:40–49)

PASS THE BUTTER, PLEASE.

Abigail once saved her entire family with a payment of food that included

200

loaves of bread. (1 Samuel 25:18–35)

To Egypt

Joseph and Mary ran away with baby Jesus to Egypt to escape a murderous king. They knew about the king because of a dream Joseph had!

(Matthew 2:13–14)

53

After **Jonathan's** death, his son **Mephibosheth** was injured and couldn't walk. **KING DAVID,** Jonathan's friend, took care of Mephibosheth **FOR THE REST OF HIS LIFE.**

(2 Samuel 4:4, 9:3–7)

NAAMAN

was healed from leprosy, a skin disease, by dipping himself in the **Jordan River** **7** times.

(2 Kings 5:14)

David's nephew
JONATHAN

once killed a giant who had

12

fingers and

12

toes!

(2 Samuel 21:20–21)

When **Elisha** and his friends were served a **poisonous stew,** Elisha **tossed** some **flour** into the pot and saved everyone's **LIFE!**

(2 Kings 4:40–41)

Delilah cut off all of **Samson's hair** while **he was sleeping.** When he woke up, his **strength was gone!**

(Judges 16:19)

58

Heads up!
KING UZZIAH'S
workers INVENTED
machines for
shooting ARROWS
and launching STONES
from TALL TOWERS.

(2 Chronicles 26:1,15)

Just hangin' out!

When his mule ran under an oak tree, **Absalom's** thick hair got caught in its branches. The mule ran off and left him **dangling there.**

(2 Samuel 18:9)

The prophet **Elijah** once lived **by a stream** where **ravens** delivered food to him every morning and evening.

(1 Kings 17:5–6)

As a **reward** for her dancing, **Herod's stepdaughter,** **SALOME,** was given the head of **John the Baptist** on a platter!

(Matthew 14:6–11)

JOSEPH

made his brothers **angry** when he told them about some **dreams** he had where they **BOWED DOWN TO HIM.** But his dreams **came true** years later, and his brothers **DID BOW TO HIM!**

(Genesis 37:5–11; 42:6)

When a **huge army** came to **capture** Elisha, **God** made them all blind.

(2 Kings 6:18)

64

King **Solomon** had **700 wives,** but the Bible only names **3 of his kids.** (1 Kings 11:3)

Joash

was only

7 years old

when he was

crowned king.

(2 Kings 11:21)

The wise men

who brought gifts to **baby Jesus** were **astrologers** who studied the stars and planets.

(Matthew 2:1–2, 9–11)

Nice kitty!
DANIEL
was **thrown** into a **den filled** with **hungry lions,** but they didn't hurt him.

(Daniel 6:16–22)

SWITCHING SIDES!

DAVID had **23 ELITE WARRIORS** who could **shoot arrows** or **sling stones** with **EITHER HAND.**

(1 Chronicles 12:1–7)

Can you spell that, please?

Isaiah's son

Maher-shalal-hash-baz

has the **longest name** in the Bible.

(Isaiah 8:3)

One day when

JOHN THE BAPTIST

was **preaching,** he called his listeners

a bunch of snakes.

How rude!

(Luke 3:7)

HANDS OFF!

Uzzah instantly dropped dead

after touching the ARK of

the COVENANT.

(2 Samuel 6:6–7)

Sarah was **90** years old when she had her **first baby.**

(Genesis 17:17)

After one year of beauty treatments, **ESTHER** was chosen to become **QUEEN** of Persia.

(Esther 2:12–17)

Jeremiah once hid his underwear in a rock by the river for several days!

(Jeremiah 13:4–6)

Queen Esther risked her life by going to see her husband, King Ahasuerus, without an invitation.

(Esther 4:11, 16)

DO NOT ENTER
WITHOUT
INVITATION

Check the GPS!

Abram was

75

when he and his wife,
Sarai, set out on a

500-MILE

HIKE TO FIND A NEW HOME.

(Genesis 12:4–6)

When **KING BELSHAZZAR** threw a **HUGE FEAST** for **1,000** friends, a **mysterious hand** appeared from nowhere and wrote a **message** on the **WALL.**

(Daniel 5:1–5)

John the Baptist lived **in the desert,** wore clothes made of **camel's hair,** and ate **locusts** and **wild honey.**

(Mark 1:4, 6)

Shadrach, Meshach, and Abednego were tied up and thrown into a blazing fire, but they didn't get burned!

(Daniel 3:23–26)

GOD put a **SPECIAL MARK** on **CAIN** so no one would **EVER** KILL HIM.

(Genesis 4:15)

WHAT'S THAT SMELL?

A woman once **dumped** an **entire bottle** of **expensive perfume** on **Jesus'** head.

(Mark 14:3)

TWELVE MEN

were in a **house together** when flames **SUDDENLY** appeared. The flames **rested** on **each man** and they were **ABLE TO SPEAK** in **languages** they had **NEVER LEARNED!**

(Acts 2:2–4)

Jeremiah was thrown into a **muddy pit** after **telling people** things they didn't want to hear. He sank down **SO FAR**, it took **four men** to pull him out!

(Jeremiah 38:6, 10)

Two brothers named **James** and **John** were known as **"SONS OF THUNDER!"**

(Mark 3:17)

Now you see him, now you don't!

PHILIP

was once instantly **transported** about 20 miles!

(Acts 8:38–40)

The Bible says  had brothers and sisters. The names of his brothers were

James,

Joses,

Judas,

and

Simon.

(Mark 6:3)

It's a bird? A plane? No, it's a . . . scroll!

Zechariah
the prophet once saw **a flying scroll** that was **30 FEET LONG** and **15 FEET WIDE!**

(Zechariah 5:1–2)

Lydia,
the only **female business owner** mentioned in the New Testament, **sold purple cloth.**

(Acts 16:14)

Lot once made **DINNER FOR TWO ANGELS.** What food would you **serve to angels?**

(Genesis 19:1–3)

Lost and found!

When **Jesus** was **12 years old,** his parents accidentally **left him behind** for

3 days

after a family trip to Jerusalem!

(Luke 2:41–46)

Zaccheus

was so short that he had to climb a tree to see Jesus over people's heads.

(Luke 19:2-4)

Tubal-Cain

is the first person mentioned in the Bible who made

TOOLS.

(Genesis 4:22)

The FIRST babysitter!

Miriam watched over her **baby brother** while he **floated in a basket** on the river.

(Exodus 2:4)

A priest named **Zechariah** doubted the angel **Gabriel's** message that he **would have a son.** So the angel made Zechariah **unable to speak** until the baby was born.

(Luke 1:19–20)

Paul was in a **terrible shipwreck.** He washed ashore on an island and was **bitten by a venomous snake.**

But he lived to **tell about it!**

(Acts 27:27–28:5)

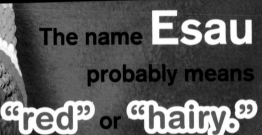

When **Esau** was born, he was **red all over**

AND COVERED WITH HAIR.

The name **Esau** probably means **"red"** or **"hairy."**

(Genesis 25:25)

After **Judas Iscariot** died, **MATTHIAS** was **CHOSEN** as the **TWELFTH APOSTLE** by **casting lots.** (Casting lots is a game similar to rolling dice or drawing straws.)

(Acts 1:26)

Kids rule!

Jesus **scolded** his disciples when they tried to keep children from bothering him.

(Matthew 19:14)

Smackdown!

Jacob limped

for the rest of his life after wrestling all night with a man he didn't know.

(Genesis 32:24–31)

KING HEROD AGRIPPA died suddenly
while giving a speech and was immediately
EATEN BY WORMS.
Yuck!

(Acts 12:21–23)

Queen Athaliah, who reigned for **6 YEARS,** was the **only woman** in the Bible to rule over the kingdoms of **Israel** or **Judah.**

(2 Kings 11:1–3)

Hurray!

When **Mary** visited her cousin **Elizabeth,** the **baby** in Elizabeth's belly was **so happy,** he **jumped for joy!**

(Luke 1:41, 44)

PAUL
and SILAS

were chained up in prison.
In the middle of the night,

their chains fell off

and the prison doors

flew open!

(Acts 16:23–26)

Adam and Eve were the first eco-friendly fashion designers. They made their own clothes out of fig leaves.

(Genesis 3:7)

PEEK·A·BOO!

Baby **Joash** was

hidden in a bedroom

to keep him safe from a

wicked queen.

He stayed there for

6 years.

(2 Kings 11:2–3)

PHOTO CREDITS

EXPERIENCE THE BOOK
THAT SHAPES HISTORY

Museum of the Bible is a 430,000-square-foot building located in the heart of Washington, D.C.—just steps from the National Mall and the U.S. Capitol. Displaying artifacts from several collections, the Museum explores the Bible's history, narrative, and impact through high-tech exhibits, immersive settings, and interactive experiences. Upon entering, you will pass through two massive, bronze gates resembling printing plates from Genesis 1. Beyond the gates, an incredible replica of an ancient artifact containing Psalm 19 hangs behind etched glass panels. Come be inspired by the imagination and innovation used to display thousands of years of biblical history.

Museum of the Bible aims to be the most technologically advanced museum in the world, starting with its unique Digital Guide that allows guests to personalize their museum experience with navigation, customized tours, supplemental visual and audio content, and more.

For more information and to plan your visit, go to
museumofthe**Bible**.org.